THE SONG OF THE PEARL

An Essay AboutSteinbeck's Short Novel , The Pearl

Wesley W. Stillwagon

The Song Of The Pearl
Wesley Stillwagon

Copyright © 2019, Wesley W. Stillwagon.

Wesley W. Stillwagon, Sr. is a retired training manager and senior instructional designer engaged in such corporations and partnerships as RCA (four divisions), Loral Electronic Mainstream Access, Pennsylvania Electric (Penelec), New Jersey Blue Cross and Blue Shield, and KPMG Peat Marwick, LLP, He is a Steinbeck/Ricketts Scholar and has many publications regarding training management and the work of John Steinbeck.

Table of Contents

Abstract

John Steinbeck's The Pearl includes many references to songs that accompany the perceptions of a central character named, Kino. It is important to note that the writer used the term 'song" and as such implied something greater than a single musical note, chord, or phrase. He was referring to a streaming complex of feeling tones -- a melody or song. Such streaming influences from the unconscious may impact an individual's perception, judgment, decisions, and conclusions often before they are able to explain their reaction. While many can relate to such experiences, understanding the source and purpose could enrich the experience. How the unconsciously inspired influences impact us depends upon our individual adult maturity, functional style, and attitude. An example of such influences are regularly employed in film and stage plays. To unify an influence among individual audience members, a well developed film or stage play's musical score serves to bring together audience feeling tones to support a scene. It may dramatically increase the viewing experience across a wide range of individual styles. This essay introduces the conceptual tools to build an understanding and appreciation for such influences. The essay could be used as supporting evidence for greater funding for the arts in education.

1

Steinbeck, Jung The Pearl

John Steinbeck had a scholarly interest in the work of Swiss Psychiatrist, Carl G. Jung. Years before confirming this fact, I theorized the connection from story line, character depth, and language. The strongest evidence was found in the non-fiction work, The Sea Of Cortez, co-authored by Steinbeck and his marine biologist friend, Edward Flanders Ricketts. Ricketts was the model for "Doc" in Cannery Row, Sweet Thursday, and other Steinbeck characters. Steinbeck's interest in Jung was confirmed later in biographies.

It appears to me that Steinbeck's Jung interest began in earnest in about 1922 when he was befriended by the popular, independent, and brilliant philosophy chair at Stanford University, Harold Chapman Brown during in formal discussions at the Brown residence. It is difficult to confirm this as the availability of Brown's papers and publications is very limited. It is my opinion that Brown and Jung both respected the work of Harvard professor, William James and agreed on the importance of bringing science together with philosophy to the benefit of humanity.

John Steinbeck's short novel, "The Pearl" describes the real and symbolic impact a found, large, and valuable pearl had on individuals and the citizens of a small Mexican coastal community. In particular the story follows a young family and describes how the jewel becomes a catalyst for unwelcomed change. This is similar to many myths, fables, and legends but presented with the advantage of Steinbeck's exceptional journalism influence on the creation of a novel.

The Pearl and the Song

"Kino heard the little splash of morning waves on the beach. It was very good—Kino closed his eyes again to listen to his music. Perhaps he alone did this and perhaps all of his people did it. His people had once been great makers of songs so that everything they saw or thought or did or heard became a song (Steinbeck, 1947). The Pearl, Page 5, Kindle Edition.

The central character of The Pearl is Kino, a young father with a loving wife and a new born son who lived very frugally on income from fishing, pearl diving, and whatever opportunities arose to provide a meager income. They were a poor but otherwise happy family.

When I read about Kino's perceptions being accompanied by songs, I thought this was a higher evolved individual than I would have expected among an aboriginal community. I justified my conclusion because he seemed more conscious of his perceptions and as such he seemed capable of better decision making, problem-solving, and logical or value judgments. Among tribes, such qualities are usually found only in the tribal medicine man, worman, or chief. He enjoyed success determined not by accumulated wealth but based upon intellectual capabilities. He was a man capable of seeing more of the big picture inside and outside than I would have expected among aboriginal social groups.

The Song and Feeling Tones

Kino had wise man qualities of myth and legend. Such character qualities were also displayed in Tom Joad in Steinbeck's The Grapes of Wrath and Doc" of Cannery Row and Sweet Thursday. None of them wealthy in resources but who consistently displayed they were men of honor, charity, and decency. None were particularly religious in the traditional sense yet they were humans who could be trusted because they were socially responsible and clearly saw their contribution to their family, their community and who acted with that better standard of humanity. Their behavior and accomplishments demonstrated an awakening to their Ego and as a result were able to distinguish their uniqueness

There is no way to confirm but the songs that accompanied Kino's perceptions consisted of more than a single note, a chord, line, or a simple musical phrase. But perhaps intuitively, it had all of the musical qualities of a complex composition or arrangement. It may have included a prelude, a melody, major chords, counterpoint, and a finale. Perhaps we are all born with this ability but haven't recognized its role in our cognition. There is no way of telling if Kino had any music education or even some exposure sufficient to create a song that was related to an object, a person, or an event.

Many of us experience a feeling tone when we perceive an object, individual, or subject and I am guessing this may be what Kino experienced. Perhaps it is the internally inspired music that enables the libido to sort out a single item or person among hundreds for us to focus upon. It may be the source of psychic energy applied to the object or person that raises its image above the threshold of consciousness, or relates it to the Ego. The background music in films and plays are meant to augment or induce individual reaction to the scene, individual, or object. The popular film, The Bad News Bears, utilized classical music very effectively throughout the film. Such practices are found in many popular films. Allegro No.! by Adolf Minot is still appropriate for a chase scene; Brahm's Waltz or Romance by Frederick A. Williams (Op. 88) for romantic love scenes.

A film, stage play, or tel-a-play's background music is intended to inspire the viewer's value or feeling functions to suit the mood or emotion of the scene, actor, object, or subject. And the right music behind the scene seems universally appealing – across all cultures and languages. Masters of film original score such as Vangelis (The Conquest of Paradise), Jerry Goldsmith, (Rudy), Randy Edelman (Gettysburg) and Rachel Portman, (The Cider House Rules) I felt did a superb job matching the score to the dramatic scene. And we are fortunate to see other such masters of matching the mood, or song to the scene. Regarding television programming, Richard Rogers, Victory At Sea series was highly acclaimed for the musical score in the 1950s. Regarding Rogers, series score, a reviewer once stated, the music often was the only thing needed to support the visual presentation. I often theorized that segments of Schubert's Prelude in Gb minor could be used in a film play for several scenes including romantic and adventure, but that's merely my opinion.

A film's musical score is used to project uniform feeling tones on the scene to aid the evaluation (feeling) of audience members.

In Jung's analytical psychology, the feeling tones or music is a product of the psyche's feeling or value function, one of two rational judgment functions, the other being thinking. Scientific psychology confines "thinking" as a function of logic, planning, naming, and social considerations. It is not, as commonly believed, used to name all cognitive processes that seem to be going on in the head.

Jung describes "feeling tones":

"The process of evaluation is different. The fire I see arouses emotional reactions of a pleasant or unpleasant nature, and the memory-images thus stimulated bring with them concomitant emotional phenomena which are known as feeling-tones. In this way an object appears to us as pleasant, desirable, and beautiful, or as unpleasant, disgusting, ugly, and so on. In ordinary speech this process is called feeling." C. G. Jung, The Structure and Dynamics of the Psyche, (1960, C. G. Jung, CW8.P 141), Princeton.

A single note played on a piano may not produce a conscious feeling tone. By conscious, I mean the object or subject has reached enough psychic energy or the necessary threshold to relate to the Ego. An object or subject must relate to the Ego to become conscious. The Ego is the psychy object that includes the content of all we are currently aware. The note with the appropriate chord (C, E, Bb,G) may produce a conscious feeling tone. If it does, it also produces a value judgment unique to the individual perceiving it. Kino's reaction to the pearl was dramatically different from the wealthy physician who would not treat Kino's baby following the scorpion sting. The physician and Kino's history or previous experiences with such things are very different and therefore produces different feeling tones or songs unique to the individual. If the note and chord were played along a sequence to produce a composition it may produce a value judgment especially when paired with a visual or audible external or internal experience. The feeling tone brings a form of rationality to a perception. It should be noted that if the reaction to an event, object, or individual, produces no feeling tone, or song, it is still a neutral value judgment.

2

Individual Perception

How we react to reading The Pearl depends a lot upon who we are as individuals – our perspective, style, attitude, history, and our adult maturity determine the value of a personal reading experience. Personally I find Steinbeck's work plays to me better than other writers and given the millions of Steinbeck books sold around the world in many languages, even decades after his death serves as evidence of global agreement. I have been curious about understanding the Steinbeck appeal for some time and have thought it worthy of consideration from the perspective of a non-clinical Jungian. A non-clinical Jungian is one who found Jung's work useful outside of the practice of psychoanalysis and therapy such as one engaged in improving critical skills instructional experiences.

Such a specialty would be valued in today's more individual and cognitive demanding work. The performance analysis tools used in the days of mass production such as time and motion studies are no longer useful for today's tasks. Statistically based psychological testing would not be of value in such consideration either as performance becomes more of a result of individual effort. John Steinbeck found Carl Jung's Analytical Psychology useful in his work. Understanding such things requires different concepts, models, and language to understand the unique individual -- a subject quite different from the statistical norm.

"Is" or Non Teleogical Cognition

I know I am asking the reader to consider a different perspective in judging what I have written. To some, what I've stated may fall outside the realm of traditional science. But Jung, Steinbeck, and Ricketts were empiricists of the truist sense. I believe one must remember that science is a tool to establish truth and not the truth itself. Analytical Psychology uses the same analytical method as nuclear physic; that is, analytical research. This is research based upon what the object of research does without concern for how it does it. It is a form of non-teleogical cognition or "is cognition" (referred to as "is thinking" by Steinbeck and Ricketts in the Log From The Sea of Cortez. Steinbeck and Ricketts were using the term "thinking" in the common sense. Since I prefer distinguishing the term as the judgment function that employs logic, planning, and social considerations to arrive at a conclusion or judgment, the term cognition better describes the work of all of the perception, judgment, and aperception functions of the psyche.

In the Introduction to "The Log From The Sea Of Cortez, credit for the concept of "is thinking (cognition)" goes to Ed Rickets:

> "Though Ricketts read widely and was extraordinarily knowledgeable, his worldview was narrow in that it was essentially Eastern and mystical. Indeed, what he called nonteleological or "is" thinking is essentially noncausal thinking. His major thirst in life was to see and to understand, which he defined as "breaking through" Introduction to the Log From The Log From The Sea of Cortez, (1941, J Steinbeck, E. Ricketts location 281) Penguin, Kindle Edition,.

Many western traditional scientists believe the Chinese had no science perhaps because of their holistic perspective on research rather than a western linear, perspective, but a review of their accomplishments like creation of explosive powder, acupuncture, and other medical advances should dispel that belief. Some traditional scientists believe that all science must fall within a cause and effect constraint. Non-teleogical research and cognition does not agree with this stipulation in its research Analytical psychology is comfortable with non-teleological cognition and so is nuclear physics. If Analytical psychology is dismissed for analytical research so too must be the findings in nuclear physics. They both use the same technique or study procedures. Refusing to accept something as factual unless it passes a cause and effect standard is not empirically scientific at all.

3

The Cognition Process

To understand how Kino was influenced by the song of the pearl may require abandoning a confining cause and effect conceptual box. One may have to step out of that box and open his or her mind to prejudgment free perception. In doing so the often competing perception and judgment functions cease their battle for attention. Perception is allowed to dominate the processes because they are now free from value or logic influences once the perception goal is satisfied. Even the libido has lost its influence in modifying the image that relates to the ego -- it has ceased to project upon the object under consideration and as a result the senses are enhanced and intuition has free play in the cognitive processes.

The process began in Kino's case through his eyes when he discovered (sensed) the pearl. Eyesight is one of the senses we use to determine if something is or is not. The image that played upon the optic nerve of his eye is not the exact image perceived, becomes conscious or relatede to the Ego. All images must relate to the ego to become a conscious perception.

Kino's unconscious determined the pearl "IS," through eyesight (one of the five senses). The image is still unconscious. At this instance, it was not named, given a purpose, fit into a plan or a scheme. These things were accomplished by through a process called apperception; that is, the psyche's thinking function in concert with the feeling function, named it, considered it logically, placed it in a plan, determined its value, applied what was learned or inherited from personal experience, and perhaps the experiences of all of Kino's ancestors with such objects. It also raised its psychic energy sufficient to relate to the ego and become conscious.

Regarding the cognitive process in play, Jung said:

"Consciousness seems to stream into us from outside in the form of sense-perceptions. We see, hear, taste, and smell the world, and so are conscious of the world. Sense-perceptions tell us that something is. But they do not tell us what it is. This is told us not by the process of perception but by the process of apperception, and this has a highly complex structure. Not that sense-perception is anything simple; only, its complex nature is not so much psychic as physiological. The complexity of apperception, on the other hand, is psychic. We can detect in it the cooperation of a number of psychic processes. Supposing we hear a noise whose nature seems to us unknown. After a while it becomes clear to us that the peculiar noise must come from air-bubbles rising in the pipes of the central heating: we have recognized the noise. This recognition derives from a process which we call thinking. Thinking tells us what a thing is."Jung, The Structure and Dynamics of the Psyche, CW. 8, Page 140, Pub Princeton.

Kino's pearl image went first into the unconscious. Some psychologists believe the unconscious is empty. In analytical psychology, unlike the Freudian Psyche model resembling an inverted pyramid, Jung's psyche is like an upright pyramid with the persona or the image we project to others (as well as the image perceived by them) at the tip, followed by the Ego, followed by the personal unconscious, and then the collective unconscious. Since the unconscious – some believe the content is not related to the Ego, it is unknowable but may be analytically determined for instance using word association tests (developed by Jung), galvanic skin analysis (lie detector), free association analysis such as the Rorschach or ink blot survey.

The song perceived by Kino's melody, its rhythm, dynamics, and rubato may be strongly modified by unconscious influences. The song's appearance was not a product of Kino's will – he did not call it up from the unconscious—he was a victim of the musical or evaluation perception. The song was a key factor in Kino's evaluating the pearl and preceded naming it and defining its purpose and social impact, which are products of his unconscious thinking function. It is similar to the streaming of modern communication technology.

Most of us who have awakened to the external and internal world can perceive an attractive musical chord or melody and clearly distinguish it from those that make us uncomfortable. This seems to be a universal, built in ability even at birth. Take for instance the chord I presented earlier, C, E, G, Bb. Most of us can perceive this is a chord (C7) that needs to be resolved. By playing the C7 chord on a keyboard followed by C major (by eliminating the Bb) it has been satisfactorily resolved. The move from a C7 chord to a C chord has a rational quality only explainable analytically. I don't believe this is something that has to be learned by many and is a built in function within the psyche. The move from C7 to C major was a rational move. Rational is not confined to the thinking function in analytical psychology.

We can only theorize the songs that accompanied Kino's perceptions. Likewise we can only guess at how they contribute to his judgments and conclusions. Perhaps we would have to wait to see what he does or accomplishes as a result. The songs may heavily influence his perceptions, judgments, and conclusions they may not outweigh his logic. The songs or feeling tones (evaluation) may have sufficient strength to dominate or most heavily influence the cognition processes.

For our analytical psychology considerations, we limit the psyche's functional cognitive processes to (perception) Sensation and Intuition, and (Judgment) Feeling and Thinking. The cognitive processes are further influenced by the individual's attitude; that is, if they are objective oriented (Extraverted) or subjective oriented (Introverted). When a psychological function and attitude are usually employed in dealing with issues and problems, this determines our psychological type. We are all born with all functions and both attitudes but with one or more emphasized over the others. Keep in mind that there rarely, if ever, a sensation without a corresponding feeling tone or thinking generated word or name, or an intuition without a corresponding thought or evaluation.

Based upon my reading (and re reading) of The Pearl, I theorize that Kino was a fairly lowly evolved Introverted Intuitive Feeling type and here's why. His reactions to the Pearl of the World as expressed to his wife were about how it would impact the future. If he were an intuitive his time reference would be spread out over the future. If he were sensation feeling type his thoughts would have been in the immediate. The senses operate in the immediate time frame. Intuition operates in a wider time frame.

4

Psychology, the (Steinbeck) Phalanx) or the Collective Psyche

One thing that sort of disappointed me in The Pearl was Steinbeck's failure to acknowledge the tribal mentality of indigenous people. Perhaps he didn't think it was relevant to the story line. A tribal mentality is common among indigenous social units especially in undeveloped countries. The bulk of the citizens share a collective psyche that has its own persona, character, and style. Steinbeck/Ricketts referred to this as the *phalanx*.

In an indigenous tribe, the bulk of the population is mainly unconscious. The word unconscious and unawake do not have the same meaning. Unconscious in this case refers to the individual being unaware of the universe about them beyond what is needed to sustain basic survival like food, shelter, safety, sex. They sometimes even have difficulty determining if they are awake or in a dream state. Not to say that a psyche isn't present within them – it is, but it is the collective psyche (phalanx) of the tribe. Their behavior isn't directed by individual will but by the phalanx of the tribe. In MOB behavior, the individual participant abandons his or her will to the phalanx of the MOB and it may cause actions far outside an individual's moral standards.

> "The universal similarity of human brains leads to the universal possibility of a uniform mental functioning. This functioning is the collective psyche. Inasmuch as there are differentiations corresponding to race, tribe, and even family, there is also a collective psyche limited to race, tribe, and family over and above the "universal" collective psyche. To borrow an expression from Pierre Janet,6 the collective psyche comprises the parties inférieures of the psychic functions, that is to say those deep-rooted, well-nigh automatic portions of the individual psyche which are inherited and are to be found everywhere, and are thus impersonal or suprapersonal." C. G. Jung, Two Essays On Analytical Psychology, CW 7, Page 235 Pub Princeton

Steinbeck presented Kino as an individual just awakening into consciousness and beginning the process of distinguishing himself from the world. He was building an Ego. Prior to this he was part of the unconscious or collective psyche. Our lives seem to be part of a process for achieving this end. The schema for individual evolvement follows.

How Kino and other residents of the village perceived and judged the Pearl of the World depended in considerable measure upon who they were – their psychological factors, their maturity as human individuals, and their attitudes. The fact that Kino was able to witness the pearl with its value, including monetary, and what it could do for him and his little family, and the risks and danger presented with its possession tells us a lot about Kino and for that reason, I theorized Kino was an introverted intuitive feeling type of individual with judgment (feeling) the primary function and intuition the auxiliary function.

5

Psychological Funtions
and Functional Types

Here are the functions and the resulting types and their impact upon individual attitudes, perception and judgment:

Sensation Function

Just like a complicated industrial control system used in robotics and such, the human psyche has information gathering functions or sub-systems. If you examine the components and functions of the typical information gathering features of a control system, you would find there are two general types. One type is very binary in its response to the system and limited to the immediate. It has a "what's happening now" quality. The limit switch is perhaps the most frequently used example of the binary, on-off sensor used in industrial control systems. Functionally, the limit switch has no ability to maintain a history of previous actions, and in human terms, is therefore only aware of the situation here and now. It is strictly an "is" or 'is not' right now determining device.

Another type of sensor is the analog. it is influenced in a human by the feeling function or tone. With the technical evolvement from an analog to digital based circuitry, power requirements, and considerable reduction in space requirements, it is now the preferred concept in control systems design. With the analog type of sensor, the control system can make decisions based upon more information than mere existence or non-existence of a target object. It can tell how close or intense the object. With an appropriate logic system, these sensors can 'evaluate' the condition against predetermined standards. Still, the information gathering has an immediate quality; the sensor, binary or analog, cannot act based upon a history or plan unless preprogrammed. It cannot evaluate on its own initiative. In an individual human psyche, the value judgment would be influence via a feeling (evaluation) tone. Expressed over a period of time with a perceptable rythm, it may be considered a song.

The sensors upon which our psyche depend have the same qualities. Binary and analog sensors (sensors coupled with judgment sub-systems) allow the psyche to determine if objects are, are not, how much, or the intensity.

The 'touch' sense helps the psyche determine the existence or non-existence of the object of touch and the intensity of the touch. Our eyes determine the existence of color and the intensity when paired with the judgment functions (Feeling and Thinking). All senses are capable of transmitting information in terms of the immediate.

It is important to remember the time quality of the sensory function of the psyche. This knowledge will help you distinguish between sensory perceptions and intuitive or intuition perceptions.

It is also important to consider all of the senses in learning to appreciate the scope of the human psyche. Basic psychology textbooks have excellent descriptions of the sensory functions of the human psyche including very detailed accounts of how sensitive they are. They do not mention, for obvious reasons, the relationship of these functions to the time frame or the judgment functions (thinking or feeling). Cases where a sensation reaching the threshold of consciousness (relating to the Ego) automatically include a thought or feeling. Even a neutral feeling tone is a legitimate evaluation conclusion.

Since the modern basic psychology text book goes into excellent detail on the sensation function, I won't dwell upon it now, except to point out the missing relationship to time and the other functions. After all the psyche is a very sophisticated complex system, right?

I suggest, if you haven't had the opportunity to review a Psychology 101 text book recently, do so. Review the section on the sensation faculties of the human psyche. The Senses are the keyboard for communicating with the psyche, therefore the understanding of the features and limitations is essential to building knowledge in a scientific psychology.

Jung used the following definition, which I think you will find useful in developing an understanding of the function:

"I regard sensation as one of the basic psychological functions.... Sensation is the psychological function that mediates the perception of a physical stimulus. It is, therefore, identical with perception. Sensation must be strictly distinguished from feeling, since the latter is an entirely different process, although it may associate itself with sensation as "feeling-tone." Sensation is related not only to external stimuli but to inner ones, i.e., to changes in internal organic process." C. G. Jung, Psychological Types CW 6, Page 462, Pub Princeton

William James said the following of sensation and perception:

"The words Sensation and Perception do not carry very definitely discriminated meanings in popular speech, and in Psychology also their meanings run into each other. Both of them name processes in which we cognize an objective world; both (under normal conditions) need the stimulation of incoming nerves ere they occur; Perception always involves Sensation as a portion of itself; and Sensation in turn never takes place in adult life without perception also being there. The nearer the object cognized comes to being a simple quality like 'hot,' 'cold,' 'red,' 'noise,' 'pain,' apprehended irrelatively to other things, the more the state of mind approaches pure sensation. The fuller of relations the object is, on the contrary; the more it is something classed, located, measured, compared, assigned to a function, etc., etc.; the more unreservedly do we call the state of mind a perception, and the relatively smaller part in it which sensation plays.

Sensation, then, so long as we take the analytic point of view, differs from Perception only in the extreme simplicity of its object or content. Its function is that of mere acquaintance with a fact. Perception's function, on the other hand, is knowledge about a fact; and this knowledge admits of numberless degrees of complication. But in both sensation and perception we perceive the fact as an immediately present outward reality (underlines by author), and this makes them different from 'thought' and 'conception,' whose objects do not present in this immediate physical way."

"...Most books start with sensations, as the simplest mental facts and proceed synthetically, constructing each higher stage from those below it. But this is abandoning the empirical method of investigation. No one ever had a simple sensation by itself. Consciousness, from our natal day, is of a teeming multiplicity of objects and relations, and what we call simple sensations are results of discriminative attention, pushed to a very high degree." William James: The Principles of Psychology, Vol. 2, Page 5, Pub Dover

The product of the sensation function are senses outputted to the unconscious.

Sensation Functional Type

"No other human type can equal the extraverted (object oriented) sensation type in realism. His sense for objective facts is extraordinarily developed. His life is an accumulation of actual experiences of concrete objects, and the more pronounced his type, the less use does he make of his experience..." C. G. Jung, Psychological Types, CW 6, Page 363, Pub. Princeton.

In the "forest for the trees" allegory, the sensation types are the experts in bark and leaf patterns. Their world is made up of forgotten experiences assembled in the quest of object details. Because the details of the object are most important, no time is left for the analysis of the connection between the object and other objects. Time-wise, they are only interested in the here and now and have little to spare for plans, historical evidence, long term schemes, or the big picture.

Perception is an end product of sensation or the other perceptive function, intuition. They both are the information gathering functions of the psyche. When combined with existing knowledge, memory and etc, or apperception the result, if sufficient psychic energy exists to relate to the ego, then a perception is formed. Since the Sensation Type individual has developed the Sense function so well through years of practice, the information gathered through the sense will be near detail complete. Since they are interested foremost in the here and now, the knowledge they will apply to the sensory signal to form the perception will be, depending upon the adult development of the individual, skewed heavily toward details and a very narrow time frame. The image that comes to consciousness is correspondingly modified according to this detailed, narrow time perspective. The logical and value judgments developed with the thinking and feeling functions will also reflect this one-sided perspective. Usually, one of the two rational functions (thinking or feeling) is habitually relied upon by the sensor over the other, with the expected behavioral results.

The judgment activities of the sensation type, are likewise colored by the detail and rapidly influenced knowledge and perceptions. More important would be the noticeable lack of patience for the judgment processes, or those who would dare to carefully use them.

The sensation type seldom has difficulty in reaching or making a decision. They can and will do so with the speed unmatched by any other types. We must remember, contained within that benefit may be the loss of the quality of the decision due to the speed with which it was reached, although it may not be a bad idea to follow a sensation type into a field of battle.

The action resulting from the speedy decision could also be defined as impulsiveness.

You will see, especially after you've read and began to apply some of these concepts, that there are positive and negative sides to every type. The distinction between the types will be less noticeable with the adult development of the individual. The more developed they are, the more they have integrated their weaker functions. The more those functions are integrated the better their problem solving and life living skills. As a trainer, preparing men and women to handle the unexpected, we may be obliged to present challenges that develop an individual's weaker functions. Team building should include instructions in functional types to build appreciation for individual player contribution and proper role assignments.

John Steinbeck's marine biologist friend, Edward Flanders Ricketts was an Introverted Sensing Feeling type and I suspect that judgment (Feeling) was the dominant function because of his sympathies and courtesies for other people. I think this is open for debate.

Feeling Function

The term 'feeling' impacts us all with slight differences. To some, it describes the pleasant or unpleasant muscle reaction in the pit of our stomach, to others, it describes irrationality. It even connotes more feminine images in some people. Some of us are more uncomfortable in expressing feelings than others, perhaps considering this a sign of weakness. However, to really understand the psychology of The Song of the Pearl, we have to agree on a suitable feeling definition that will stand on its own and fit well into the model we are describing.

The suffering of our society from the lack of understanding and appreciation of the feeling function is great. The male of our species, with its current emphasis on the 'macho,' the numerous personally devastating complexes, neurosis, and failures in relationship can all be tied to the ignorance of the feeling function. Perhaps the damage from this ignorance even extends to diplomatic failures between nations. We tend to view feeling as inferior to thinking and as irrational. We incorrectly undervalue the dynamics of the function in our decisions, sometimes going to great lengths to rationalize a strong feeling-motivated action with logical afterthoughts we pretend to be part of our pre-event plan.

Jung said:

"I count feeling among the four psychological functions. I am unable to support the psychological school that considers feeling a secondary phenomenon dependent upon 'representations' or sensations, but in company with Hoffding, Wundt, Lewhmann, Kulpe, Baldwin and others, I regard it as an independent function sui generis.

Feeling, therefore, is an entirely subjective process, which may be in every respect independent of external stimuli, though it allies itself with every sensation. Even an 'indifferent' sensation possesses a feeling-tone, namely that of indifference, which again expresses some sort of valuation. Hence feeling is a kind of judgment, differing from intellectual judgment in that its aim is not to establish conceptual relations but to set up a subjective criteria of acceptance or rejection. Valuation by feeling extends to every content of consciousness, of what ever kind it may be..." C. G. Jung, Psychological Types, CW 6, Page 433, Pub. Princeton

The Feeling Type

The feeling type enjoys the interpersonal, one-on-one experience over the social. For that reason; they are our best sales people. They are either gifted with interpersonal effectiveness at birth or seem to learn the techniques of interpersonal effectiveness very early in life. They can accurately read subtle changes in an other's faces, expressions, and body language. For these reasons, they are great communicators and advocates for a cause or mission.

While the Thinking Type relies upon facts, logic, and social influences for their judgment and conclusions, the Feeling Type seems more influenced in the interpersonal, value, and historical information.

A mistaken assumption among western cultures is that value judgment is not rational, when the opposite is true. It is subjective, but subjectivity is not a term opposed to rationality. Judgments made through the feeling function are just as rational and as important as ones developed through the thinking. Technologically advanced societies seem to have difficulty with this reality. Eastern civilizations do not.

Feeling types prefer to keep their life activity within well defined, more manageable areas like their home. Their management style is likely to be very similar to their positive attitude toward family and home. It is likely they will even state this in their description of their organization. Pictures of friends, family, and co-workers may be displayed around their office.

Kino was an Introverted Intuitive Feeling Type in my opinion based upon his reactions to events, people, objects, and experiences and the future impact on life as a result of the possession of the pearl.

Intuition Function

Another perception function available in the psyche is intuition. This function is much harder to describe for the source of the information is not obvious. Almost all of us can remember times when we had a hunch or reaction to a 'gut response and the right word occurred just at the right time. We had a hunch and we can say the psyche gathered information using the intuition function.

The intuition function appears to operate independent of time. Immediacy is the realm of our sensation function, the opposite is often true of our intuition function. Through the intuition function, we can often piece together details that our sensation function cannot perceive. More often, we are able to do so before we can successfully describe the details of the bonding element of the connection. Imagine walking quickly down a city street close to a building. As you approach the corner, there is a reaction in your abdomen telling you to 'put the brakes on.' Sure enough, a bicyclist speeds past the point of potential danger. Or, you are about to sit in an unfamiliar chair that appears safe but the word "broken" appears in your mind with an accompanying fear reaction. You examine the chair carefully and find a hidden but broken leg. These experiences, in which your psyche used information unavailable to your sensation function, were examples of intuition.

Jung says the following of the intuitive function:

"I regard intuition as a basic psychological function. It is the function that mediates perceptions in an unconscious way.... The peculiarity of intuition is that it is neither sense perception, nor feeling, nor intellectual inference, although it may also appear in these forms. In intuition, a content presents itself whole and complete, without our being able to explain or discover how this content came into existence. Intuition is a kind of instinctive apprehension, no matter of what contents." C. G. Jung, Psychological Types, CW 6, Page 453, Pub Princeton

The product of the Intuitive Function is an intuition.

Both Sensation and Intuition have the quality of being given or of happening, as opposed to, resulting from reason, logic or evaluation. Behavior resulting from response to sensation or intuition, without judgment are, therefore, by observation, irrational.

The impact of our perceptive functions upon our behavior is directly proportional to the level of consciousness we are at when they occur. I am sure this doesn't surprise you when you think about it. People taking their initial parachute jump always report how their "awareness seemed to peak, or senses become most acute, just prior to the jump." The tools of awareness are the perceptive functions sensation and intuition.

A misguided editor wrote in the Introduction to a later version of "The Log From The Sea of Cortez"

"Above all, though, the Log is a celebration of the holistic vision the authors shared, and in accordance with their "reverence" for the ideas of Allee and Ritter, this is depicted in terms more mystical and intuitive than scientific. " From the Introduction to The Log From The Sea Of Cortez, Kindle Edition, writer unspecified, Pub Penquin.

In the fascinating book about U. S. Navy Commander Joseph Rochefort, the man that led the code breaking team at Pearl Harbor the early days of World War II under Admiral Chester Nimitz. The team successfully broke Japan's Navy code, JN-25. In the biography, Rochefort was described thus:

"Rochefort was invariably "brilliant," if not actually a "genius." He was "the dean of the Navy's cryptanalysts," blessed with "a superlative memory for detail and a deep intuitive knowledge built up over years of studying Japanese naval operations." Joe Rochefort's War, Elliott Carlson, Naval Institute Press, Kindle Versio, Location 223

Likely the code breaking team, interestingly made up of many musicians from the sunken battleship California, shortened the war perhaps by years. They determined Japan's next attack on Midway Island and enabled US Naval forces to set up an ambush to fight off Japan's attack of the island. This can hardly be referred to as non-scientific or mystical. Nor would Steinbeck, Ricketts, or Joseph Campbell consider it so. They would recognize it as scientific, analytical, intuitive, and a fine example of non-teleogical cognition.

Intuition Type

The Intuitor Type, unlike the opposite, the Sensor Type with their concern for immediate detail, is comfortable facing problems from the perspective of the big picture, the future, past experiences, history, synthesis, and possibilities. Logic or value judgments are not necessarily employed with any strength in cognition either. Solutions are arrived at through a process of weighing possibilities until an intuited word or gut reaction tells them the analysis is complete. Weighing possibilities is so important in their cognition that they may be angered if someone suggests a possibility that they had not considered in the weighing process causing them to repeat the painstaking work.

Jung said of the distinction between the intuition and the sensation types,

> "Whenever intuition predominates, a peculiar and unmistakable psychology results. Because extraverted intuition is oriented by the object, there is a marked dependence on external situations, but it is altogether different from the dependence on the sensation type. The intuitive is never to be found in the world of accepted reality values, but he has a keen nose for anything new and in the making. Because he is always seeking out new possibilities, stable conditions suffocate him. He seizes on new objects or situations with great intensity, sometimes with extraordinary enthusiasm, only to abandon them cold-bloodedly, without any compunction and apparently without remembering them, as soon as their range is known and no further developments can be divined." C. G. Jung, Psychological Types, CW6, Page 368, Pub. Princeton

If there was ever any one type description used to sell Jung's Psychological Model, his description of the Extraverted Intuitive, in my opinion is the one I recommend, especially to other intuitors. I was so relieved after reading the complete description, because until I was twenty-five, I thought everyone approached problems or goals this way and was somewhat nervous when I realized they did not. I enthusiastically recommend reading Jung's "Psychological Types" to anyone truly interested in learning about themselves and their fellow human beings.

This type has the ability to find a common thread through some apparently very disconnected material or a complex. I know there is a term for the ability to visually see to the side called "peripheral vision," I believe the term "peripheral perception" would apply to this type, subsequently, ergonomic considerations for the "Sensor" type could be considerably different for the "Intuitor" with this more holistic perception ability.

As much as the Sensor lacks in diplomacy, the Intuitor makes up. They are on face value very likeable people and very competent negotiators for their innate ability to read the pulse of a population. They are capable of uncovering trends from data that Sensors and the rational types (Thinkers and Feelers) may deem meaningless.

In a complicated technical system control operation that includes many indicators, measuring meters, controls, and alarms needing attention from a competent operator, the Intuitor type could be invaluable. They would also be very good at accomplishing goals through the interpersonal such as directing or instructing outboard personnel. They have a valuable ability to uncover discord before it becomes a serious problem in work or other social situations.

Intuition and Feeling were the psychological functions employed for the songs perceived by Kino. Intuition provided the linking of the musical notes, chords, and phrases to produce the song and enhanced his vision's broad time frame in considering the pearl's potential.

Thinking Function

Thinking, the second judgmental function we shall consider, is the function that links concepts using the rules of logic and the processes related to planning and social consideration. It is our psyche's cold calculating mode with which today's linear developed technology is most comfortable. It comprises the connecting ability of numbers, meaning, formula, terms, concepts and is our function used in planning.

Jung said of thinking:

"This I regard as one of the four basic psychological functions. Thinking is the psychological function which, following its own laws, brings the contents of ideation into conceptual connection with one another. It is an apperceptive activity, and as such may be divided into active and passive thinking. Active thinking is an act of will, passive thinking is a mere occurrence. In the former case, I submit the contents of ideation to a voluntary act of judgment; in the latter, conceptual connections establish themselves of their own accord, and judgments are formed that may even contradict my intention. I may afterwards recognize their directedness through an act of active apperception. Active thinking, accordingly, would correspond to my concept of directed thinking...Passive thinking...today I would call it intuitive thinking." C. G. Jung, Psychological Types, CW 6, Page 480, Pub. Princeton.

"The term "thinking" should, in my view, be confined to the linking up of ideas by means of a concept, in other words, to an act of judgment, no matter whether this act is intentional or not..." C. G. Jung, Psychological Types, CW 6, Page 481Pub Princeton

"Thought is the specific content or material of the thinking function." C. G. Jung, Psychological Types, CW6, Page 482, Pub. Princeton

While we generally define any process that seems to go on in our head as thinking, it would be useful for the purposes of this book to confine the term to those processes we actively employ to arrive at a decision, define purpose, plan or draw a conclusion through the rules of logic.

Thinking Functional Type

C. G. Jung:

"It is a fact of experience that the basic psychological functions seldom or never all have the same strength or degree of development in the same individual. As a rule, one or the other function predominates, in both strength and development. When thinking holds prior place among the psychological functions, i.e., when the life of an individual is mainly governed by reflective thinking so that every important action proceeds, or is intended to proceed, from intellectually considered motives, we may fairly call this a thinking type..." C. G. Jung, Psychological Types, CW 6, Page 346, Pub Princeton

"...This type of man elevates objective reality, or an objectively oriented intellectual formula, into the ruling principle not only for himself but for his whole environment. By this formula, good and evil are measured, and beauty and ugliness determined. Everything that agrees with this formula is right, everything that contradicts it is wrong, and everything that passes by it indifferently is merely incidental. Because this formula seems to embody the entire meaning of life, it is made into a universal law which must be put into effect everywhere, all the time, both individually and collectively. Just as the extraverted thinking type subordinates himself to the formula, so, for their own good, everybody around him must obey it too, for whoever refuses to obey it is wrong- he is resisting the universal law, and is therefore unreasonable, immoral, and without conscience. His moral code forbids him to tolerate exceptions; his ideal must under all circumstances be realized, for in his eyes it is the purest conceivable formulation of objective reality, and therefore must also be a universally valid truth, quite indispensable for the salvation of mankind. This is not from any great love for his neighbour, but from the highest standpoint of justice and truth. Anything in his own nature that appears to invalidate this formula is mere imperfection, an accidental failure, something to be eliminated on the next occasion, or, in the event of further failure, clearly pathological..." C. G. Jung, Psychological Types, CW 6, Page 347, Pub. Princeton

Jung points out that "oughts" and "musts" are usually parts of a thinker's plan. The thinker may be guilty of attempting to force him/herself and others into one convenient mold. Of course if everyone would or could agree to such an ought or must, the thinker's plan building and rule making would be dramatically simplified with the reduction of individual human variables. I have also observed thinkers go to great lengths to convince observers or witnesses of the true but hidden logic behind their action.

Psyche Attitude

We all can be objective or goal oriented (Extraverted) or into the subjective or experience (Introverted) but when that particular psyche attitude is our default, usual, or the norm, our psychological attitude would be Introverted or Extraverted, and this means:

Estraversion

C. G. Jung:

"Extraversion is an outward-turning of libido. I use this concept to denote a manifest relation of subject to object, a positive movement of subjective interest towards the object. Everyone in the extraverted state thinks, feels, and acts in relation to the object, and moreover in a direct and clearly observable fashion, so that no doubt can remain about his position dependence upon the object. In a sense, therefore, extraversion is a transfer of interest from subject to object. If it is an extraversion of <u>thinking</u>, the subject thinks himself into the object; if an extraversion of <u>feeling</u>, he feels himself into it. In extraversion, there is a strong, if not exclusive, determination by the object. Extraversion is active when it is intentional, and passive when the object compels it, i.e., when the object attracts the subject's interest of its own accord, even against his will. When extraversion is habitual, we speak of the extraverted type." C. G. Jung, Psychological Types, CW 6, Page 427, Pub Princeton

Introversion

C. G. Jung:

"Introversion means an inward turning of <u>libido</u> in the sense of a negative relation of subject to object. Interest does not move toward the object but withdraws from it in to the subject. Everyone whose attitude is introverted thinks, feels and acts in a way that clearly demonstrates that the subject is the prime motivating factor and the object is of secondary importance. Introversion may be intellectual or emotional, just as it can be characterized by sensation or intuition. It is active when the subject voluntarily shuts himself off from the object, passive when he is unable to restore to the object the libido streaming back from it. When introversion is habitual, we speak of an introverted type." C. G. Jung, Psychological Types, CW 6, Page 452, Pub Princeton

6

Levels of Adult Maturity

Levels of Adult Maturity and the Influence of the Phalanx

In developing his phalanx concept, Steinbeck articulated two key characteristics:

A group, gathering or MOB can take on an autonomous psychology and behave in a manner that may be quite different from what would be displayed by individual members under the same circumstances.

The psychology of the group frequently appears to be in antagonistic counterpoint to the individual psychology of its human units.

I would add a third point: The higher the development or maturity of the group's individual members, the less the negative influence exerted by the MOB on the group's behavior.

The four levels listed below were inspired and expanded upon from the book, The Gnostic Jung by C. G. Jung, Selected

And Introduced by Robert A. Segal.

In the book, Segal describes levels of consciousness as described by Jung in The Seven Sermons To The Dead. In introducing the levels of consciousness, Segal said,

"At birth, according to Jung, humans are entirely unconscious. Only slowly does consciousness emerge. Because the initial human state is unconscious, unconsciousness is natural rather than, as for Freud, artificial. Where for Freud the unconscious arises out of consciousness, consciousness arises out of the unconscious." Robert A. Segal, The Gnostic Jung, Page 11-12, Pub, Princeton

I did not think the level names in the book as I think they are confusing but included them for historical purposes.

The levels of conscious development or adult maturity are fourfold:

Level 1 (Primitives) . Are almost completely unaware of their uniqueness as individuals. They have no ego as the term is used in the clinical sense—that is, the psychological object within which an individual defines himself or herself and to which all objects or subjects must attach to become conscious. Those who exist at this level lead lives that revolve around basic survival, shelter, safety, and procreation. They leave decisions on important matters up to authority figures such as a father or mother. During Jung's research among African and North American Native tribes, tribal members told him that they leave all thinking and decision-making to their tribal chief or medicine person. They could not distinguish between their dream state and conscious state. They told Jung that they thought anyone charged with the burden of thinking was crazy. They were mainly unconscious.

Level 2. (Ancients) Level 2 individuals have awaken to the differences between themselves and others. This is the beginning of the existence of their ego: their awakening to their uniqueness in the world or the universe. An individual at this level typically projects onto external gods and devils. As a result of their development they gradually learn to participate in their personal path, create goals, and use individual tools in dealing with life and its issues. But for the most part they are driven to self-serving aims with their newly discovered skills. They still are mainly unconscious.

Kino was at this development level. His projections on the pearl was indicative of that fact.

Level 3. (Moderns)To understand my description of Level 3, we must agree on the definition of the term ego used here. It should be considered to mean one's conscious image of himself or herself. When we reflect upon ourselves, the image we perceive is the ego. The term is often mistakenly used to refer to an inflated ego where the self-image of an individual exceeds reality. But in truth, the ego is the focal point to which all objects of perception must relate to become conscious. Persons at Level 3 have a nearly completely developed ego and view it as their center, denying the existence of anything about themselves outside its circumference. While the Level 3 individual denies the unconscious, they are nonetheless the victim of unconscious influences in their behavior. Examples include embarrassing slips-of-the tongue or falling in love with a person who is wrong for many reasons. They may also be victims of irrational fears or hates—the Shadow, to use another term from Carl Jung, Level 3 persons are apt to become victims of group influence the collective psyce or the MOB phalanx, however emphatically they may deny this possibility.They would also deny the influences of projections from their libido on to objects, individuals, and etc. But they are only a bit less victimized by such projections than the level two individual.

Level 4. (Contemporaries) For a variety of reasons, some painful, Level 4 individuals have awakened to the reality that there is more to themselves than realized in their ego. When this happens they become aware and curious about their newly revealed psychological territory. It usually doesn't take them long to begin the exploration of this uncharted terrain within themselves. Ideally, when they do so they will seek to integrate what they discover about themselves into their existing self-image and further build their ego on stronger ground. The previously unintegrated elements of Self found in their exploration likely were the source of many of the projections they suffered at earlier stages of their development on the way to Level 4 self-knowledge. Level 4 people are thus the most conscious and least vulnerable to negative phalanx influence. They are truly their own man or woman. Their exalted state often causes them to be targetted by those of lower development as father or mother figures. The little Norwegian village in Steinbeck's The Moon Is Down seemed to be populated by many Level three and four individuals and this made managing them by the dictator and occupying forces much more difficult.

Readers may recognize the differences in persona presented by individuals at the levels I have described. These differences can be perceived through interpersonal dialogue and interaction or through observing behavior. Strong caution must be suggested to avoid pigeon holing another and then acting on that classification. Remember, we are also responsible for the persona we perceive of others and it may be very wrong. Individuals at Level 4 (Ed Ricketts, for example) often appear peaceful, content, friendly, selfless, and kind. Those at lower levels may be more easily influenced by fear, hatred, and ignorance. The fiction of John Steinbeck, who I believe intuited this truth about humans, or acquired it through his considerable philosophical study, offers unforgettable examples of people at every level of evolution or adult human maturity.

7

The Influence of Space and Time

Over the years of my study, I've realized that individually we are here to face challenges and to grow from the lessons giving experiences. The growth plan is a response to an individual need that seems to be laid out with specific purposes to achieve individual goals. As native Americans would say, "we all have our own path around the medicine wheel. " We don't learn individual lessons by comparing ourselves and our progress with statistical averages. I

We are all impacted by the time and place we were born as was Keno and everyone in the little village so heavily influenced by the "Pearl of the World". This fact seems so obvious and yet is so ignored by literature, science, and philosophy. The space/time complex is so pervasive that it is as easy to ignore as the life sustaining presence of the sun or oxygen in the air.

The village culture, traditions, attitudes, and more's depicted by Steinbeck in The Pearl were influence by time. Time determined the level of individual consciousness, whether we were born to serve or to be served, who we are attracted to or repulsed by and our general life path and plan. Ignoring time metrics ignores important life path indicators, opportunities, and handicaps. believe knowing what I've presented in this essay can serve to improve a Steinbeck reading experience and the appreciation of life in general.

Conclusion

My wish in developing this essay was to raise awareness of Steinbeck's philosophical depth and how understanding this may enrich the reading of his fiction and non-fiction. His character descriptions were always so rich that they added to entice you into the story or journal. The conceptual tools presented here may also enrich life in general. I hope it brings the reader such gifts.

www.ingramcontent.com/pod-product-compliance
Lightning Source LLC
Chambersburg PA
CBHW020331290526
45785CB00007B/3006